Speaking of merit...
(*Sammodanīya kathā*)

by Phra Nicholas Thanissaro

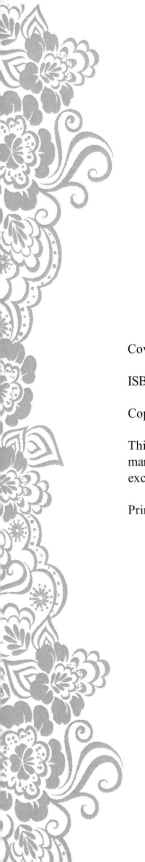

Cover design and images: © Phra Nicholas Thanissaro and Adobe Stock

ISBN (print) ISBN 978-1-09838-512-5

Printed by BookBaby Publishing in the United States of America.

Speaking of merit...
(*Sammodanīya kathā*)

by Phra Nicholas Thanissaro

Contents

In memoriam
Michael Heaton Woods
(1939-2021)

Michael Heaton Woods was born on April 22, 1939 to Dennis Arthur and Dora Olive Woods, both of whom were school teachers, in Kettering, England. He was brought up during the difficult years of rationing of the Second World War alongside one younger brother, Roger. He went to Grammar School at Kimbolton and on merit from school, was accepted into Naval Officer Training College in Dartmouth, Devon. On graduation he served his obligatory four years in the Royal Navy, in the period 1960-1965, seeing active service in the decolonization of Aden (now Yemen) and Malaya (now

Malaysia), reaching the highest rank of Lieutenant.

He married his wife Jennifer while stationed in Singapore, honeymooned in Thailand and returned to the UK for the birth of their first child 'Nicholas' (now Phra Nicholas Thanissaro), taking up civilian work in Air Traffic Control. A second child Rachel was born in 1968 and went on to become an elementary school teacher and give the family three grandsons. Michael Heaton Woods moved the family around Britain with the Air Traffic Control career every five years, stationed at various airports in England and Scotland, up until the time of his retirement when he settled in Scotland.

By nature, Michael Woods was brought up Anglican, but preferred Humanism, with a fondness for church music. His son Nicholas took ordination as a Buddhist monk in 1997. Michael and Jennifer magnanimously agreed to travel to Thailand to attend the ordination ceremony in person.

While his health allowed it during his retirement, Michael Woods was able to visit and support branches of Wat Phra Dhammakaya in the UK and Belgium, where his son had been posted, and had occasion to perform a meal offering for the monastic community of Wat Phra Dhammakaya, Manchester at their home. In around 2010, Michael Woods moved back to Harrogate, England to be closer to the hospital, suffering from Waldenstrom Macroglobulinemia and heart failure. He was looked after by his wife and daughter with annual visits from their son and allowed Buddha statues on the Dhammakaya Cetiya to be dedicated in his name during the worst bouts of illness. In later life, he showed some interest in the meditation taught by his son.

Throughout his life, Michael Woods remained fiercely independent and loved to travel, preferring peace and quiet in life – an intensely private person until the end – passing away at home, with members of his family on February 2, 2021.

Memorial services

Azusa, California
February 3-5, 2021

Silicon Valley,
California
February 5, 2021

Minneapolis, MN
February 3, 2021

Palm Beach,
Florida
February 3-5, 2021

Woking, Surrey,
UK
February 5, 2021

In Loving Memory of

Michael Heaton Woods

22nd April 1939 - 2nd February 2021

St John the Baptist Church, Knaresborough

Monday 22nd February 2021
at 12.00 noon

Knaresborough,
UK
February 22, 2021

Principles
&
Preliminaries

Principles of
Sammodanīya Kathā

This book is a stopgap aiming to provide English language oratory to facilitate something that happens every day in Theravāda Buddhist temples throughout the world – namely the ceremony for offering monastic almsfood. This ceremony needs to take place every day because without expressing gratitude for food brought to the temple in support of the monastic community, such philanthropy would soon dry up. Monks need to find a way to express heartfelt and sincere appreciation for gifts received and this usually comes in the form of a Pali language blessing and a short homily in the vernacular known as a *'sammodanīya*

kathā' (from the Mahānarada Kassapa Jātaka, lit. 'agreeable or pleasant discourses'). Even when the almsgiving takes place outside of Asia, the vernacular often continues to be limited to Thai, Burmese or Sinhala, which is disappointing for native speakers of English or the second-generation Asians who have grown up without fluency in their parents' languages.

The opportunity for English-language supporters of a temple community to understand or by inspired by the gratitude expressed by monks has been hampered not only by the language barrier but, even when attempts are made at translation, the unexplained assumptions in the message. It is with a view to bridging this gap that this book was compiled – to provide a preliminary selection of possible almsgiving homilies selected for their accessibility to English-language speaking temple supporters, some of whom will have an understanding of Buddhist principles from their upbringing, but also those who are new to Buddhist activities.

How this book was designed to be used

At branches of the Dhammakaya movement overseas, the mid-morning almsgiving ceremony has become formalized. Although some branches may follow an abbreviated version, at DIMC (Azusa) the following order of ceremonies is conducted in full:

1. MC greets the audience
2. MC leads bowing to the Buddha statue
3. MC leads bowing to the monastic community
4. MC introduces and leads the request of the Five Precepts
5. Leading monk gives the Five Precepts
6. MC introduces and leads request to offer the midday meal
7. Monastic community chant *Iti piso* / Buddha's victories / Victory protection
8. MC leads making the resolution and dedication of merit
9. Leading monk gives the almsgiving homily

10. Leading monk gives blessing in the vernacular
11. Monastic community give blessing in Pali language
12. MC leads bowing to the monastic community
13. Monastic community chant reflection on the food
14. Leading monk leads reflection on food and offering of food to the Buddha in the vernacular
15. MC leads bowing to the Buddha and concludes the ceremony

The order may differ from branch to branch and according to whether the service is held in person or online (as has been the case during the 2020-21 pandemic). This book focuses mainly on helping the MC and leading monk to find oratory for 9, 10 and 14. For completeness, the introductions for 4 and 5, and the verses for 6 and 8 have been included for aspiring MC's. My hope is that any spiritual merits arising from this work be shared for the benefit of the author's late father.

MC Script

Before requesting Five Precepts

According to the wise, keeping the precepts is the precursor, the foundation and the origin of all goodness. It is chief amongst the virtues. Keeping one's precepts pure, protects one from succumbing to all unwholesome behaviors, brings joyfulness of mind and is the harbor from which one can set sail upon the ocean toward Nirvana. Keeping the five precepts entails abstaining from killing, stealing, sexual misconduct, telling lies and using intoxicants. Thus without further ado, you are invited to request the Five Precepts together.

Requesting the Five Precepts

Mayaṃ bhante visuṃ visuṃ rakkhaṇatthāya tisaraṇena saha pañca sīlāni yācāma, dutiyaṃ pi mayaṃ bhante visuṃ visuṃ rakkhaṇatthāya tisaraṇena saha pañca sīlāni yācāma, tatiyaṃ pi mayaṃ bhante visuṃ visuṃ rakkhaṇatthāya tisaraṇena saha pañca sīlāni yācāma

Before Offering General Saṅghadāna

Generosity is one of the marks of wisdom. The discerning will choose the right time and the very best of food and drink to offer to those monks who lead a celibate life, because those monks are a 'field of merit' who yield the very highest of merit for the giver. By offering food to monks it is said that you offer five qualities of life — long life, fine complexion, good health, strength and mental acuity. Those who give will receive these qualities of life in return. Merit alone can be our refuge. Thus, without further ado, you are invited to repeat (after the congregation representative) the verses for the offering food to the monastic community together.

Offering General Saṅghadāna

Imāni mayaṃ bhante, bhattāni, saparivārāni, bhikkhusaṅghassa, oṇojayāma, sādhu no bhante, bhikkhusaṅgho, imāni, bhattāni, saparivārāni, paṭiggaṇhātu, amhākaṃ, dīgharattaṃ, hitāya, sukhāya, nibbānāya ca.

On this occasion, venerable monks, we seek your permission, to offer this food to the monastic community, together with its associated gifts. May the monastic community receive this food and these gifts from us, for our everlasting benefit, happiness and attainment of Nirvana.

<monks chant Victory protection>

At this time, I would like to invite everyone to say the verses for making the resolution.

May the food we are offering, help all of us eliminate, the defilements, from our minds.

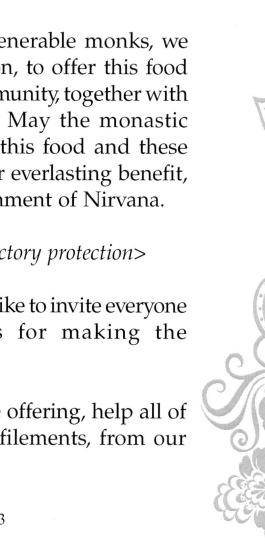

I would like to invite everyone to say the verses for dedicating merit to our late relatives.

May the merits, accumulated today, help all of our deceased relatives, to be happy in the hereafter.

At this time, I would like to invite the presiding monk to express appreciation for the midday meal and chant the blessing.

Introduction to
Sammodanīya kathā

So just before we receive our blessing today, I would like to invite everyone to close their eyes for a few moments, to recollect all the merits arising from the offering of the midday meal here at *<temple name>* today. Think of a bright clear sphere of light at the center of your body, as a place where all your merits have been gathered together – merits arising from the request of the Five Precepts, from hearing the monks chanting the verses of Victory Protection and the merits arising from the offering of the midday meal here today. *<and continue with Sammodanīya kathā at page 29, 31, 33, 37, 41, 45, 49, 51, 53, 55, 57, 61, 65, 67, 71 or 75>*

Homilies of almsgiving appreciation

1

Buddhist Symbiosis

For more than two-thousand years, the Buddhist lay and monastic communities have, in different ways, supported each other, so that members of both communities have the chance to be the very best they can be in life. The nature of the lay life is to have to work hard to earn a living, and hence to lack sufficient time to study the spiritual knowledge needed for a happy and peaceful life. The nature of the monastic life is to have to study spiritual knowledge in depth, but to lack the time to procure the basic requisites needed for life.

The solution to the problems of both communities is for monks to share their knowledge of the Dhamma, and for lay

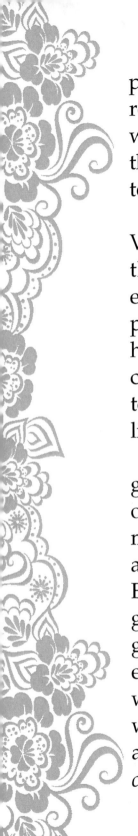

people share with the monks, the basic requisites excess to their needs. In this way both communities can be fulfilled in their vocation, while having the chance to practice generosity.

Our main teacher in Thailand, Venerable Dhammajayo, once explained this "Buddhist Symbiosis" as monks entrusting their stomachs to the lay people, while lay people entrust their hearts and minds to the monks. Both communities are consequently bound together by their reciprocal duties and can live together in peace.

Out of this arrangement comes many good things – because through the power of giving laypeople can create the meritorious energy that will attract abundance and success into their lives. Even the monks, who must be diligent in giving teachings, to repay their debt of gratitude to the laypeople, will able to expand the knowledge of Buddhist wisdom like ripples spreading wider and wider throughout world, bringing peace and enlightenment in its wake. *<and continue with 'ending' at page 81>*

2

Enduring happiness

Two-thousand five-hundred years ago, as recorded in the Aṅguttara Nikāya, the Buddha distinguished between two different sorts of happiness.

The first sort of happiness described by the Buddha, which he called *'sāmisa-sukha'* is the happiness derived from owning material possessions such as money or jewelry. A capitalist society perpetuates the myth that the more you own, the happier you will be. In reality, however, this sort of happiness is impermanent and unreliable, and in the long term will bring suffering in life when the owner is inevitably separated from those prized possessions, leaving them in a state of anxiety, worry, grief, pain or loss. This pain will one day overwhelm all the satisfaction they ever had from owning those possessions. This is why the Buddha taught us to

regard our possessions as only being 'on loan' in our lives.

The second and superior sort of happiness described by the Buddha, which he called 'nirāmisa-sukha' is happiness that comes from inside us, and which does not depend on material possessions. This sort of happiness can be attained by practice of virtues like generosity, keeping the Precepts and meditating. It is not a happiness that distracts us from our suffering, but the happiness of overcoming our suffering. It is an expansive, enduring and transformative happiness which we would want to share with others and one that will eventually pave the way for our journey toward Nirvana.

The cultivation of generosity allows us to distinguish clearly between these two forms of happiness. When the happiness of giving something away, brings more happiness than keeping it – as we have seen so clearly with the offering of the midday meal here today, this shows that you are coming close to the 'nirāmisa-sukha' or inner happiness idealized by the Buddha. *<and continue with 'ending' at page 81>*

3

Giving to the Community

The Buddha taught in the Dakkhiṇā-
vibhaṅga Sutta of the Majjhima Nikāya
that the amount of merit yielded to the
giver, by a gift to an individual – known
in Buddhism as '*paṭipuggalikadāna*', is in
proportion to the purity of the recipient.
Even if food is given to a humble animal
it will bring long-life [*āyu*], good
complexion [*vaṇṇa*], happiness [*sukha*],
strength [*bala*] and intelligence [*paṭibhāṇa*]
to the giver for no less than 100 lifetimes.
Even if the gift is given to a person who
does *not* keep the Precepts, the gift will
bring the same fruits for 1,000 lifetimes.
If the gift is given to a person who *does*
keep the Precepts the gift will bring the
same fruits for 100,000 lifetimes – and if

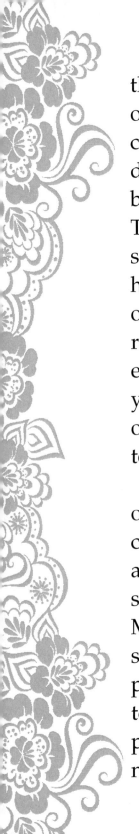

the gift is given to a hermit or ascetic outside the Buddhist monastic community who has attained some degree of mental powers, the gift will bring the same fruits for 10^{12} lifetimes. This is not to speak of a gift given to someone who is practicing for, or who has already attained sainthood at the level of stream-enterer, once-returner, non-returner, *arahant*, *paccekabuddha* or a fully-enlightened Buddha where the merit yielded is even more. These are the extent of the merits arising from offering food to an individual recipient.

But incredible as these meritorious outcomes may seem, they are still small compared with the fruits of a gift given as *'sanghadāna'* – which means 'for the sake of the whole monastic community'. Most people lack the motivation to help strangers or to give merely out of principle. They would much prefer to go to a particular temple and single out a particular monk for their attention. They need a personal connection between themselves and a monk before they will reach out with any support. They might be narrow-minded and look down on monks of low rank. Of course they still receive merit from their good deed, but it is slightly reduced from what it could be — because the merit in all of these categories of recipient cannot beat the merit from offering a gift to the community of monks.

Not only does a gift to the monastic community foster harmony amongst the monks, but it signals broad-mindedness in the giver that magnifies and multiplies the outcomes of the merit beyond what any individual gift could achieve. It is the big-heartedness of a person who does not mind which monk the monastic community delegates to receive a gift from them. Even if the community sent a novice to receive their gift they wouldn't mind. Their mind would be filled with faith before, during and after giving the gift. The Buddha taught that anyone who is sufficiently broad-minded to support the

Saṅgha in this way will receive not only many lifetimes of merit – but merit that is incalculable. *<and continue with 'ending' at page 81>*

4

Letting generosity spark joy

In the time of the Buddha, on the day of offering the Great Hall of Pubbārāma Temple, Lady Visakhā, the foremost female supporter of the Buddha, could not contain her joy and spontaneously burst into five stanzas of song to the point that the monks had to question the Buddha about this. The Buddha explained that 'my daughter Visakhā' was merely expressing the happiness she felt at succeeding, after many lifetimes, in making a great donation to the monastic community.

Our main teacher in Thailand, the Venerable Dhammajayo similarly encouraged us that when we perform any sort of meritorious deed, if we are able to fill our body, speech and mind with

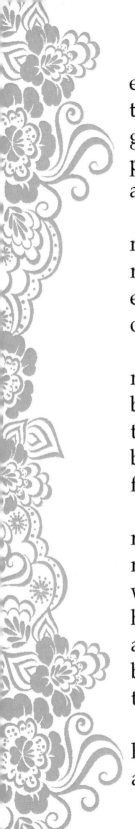

enthusiasm, it will magnify and multiply the merit, because every time we do a good deed, it will indelibly etch that positive emotion into our minds, bringing at least four clear benefits.

Firstly, whenever we think back to the merits we have done, the memory will return to us with the same joyous emotion, that will banish any regret from our mind.

Secondly, when we come to the final moments of our life, and our life flashes before us, the last image left in our mind, that will lead us to a new existence, will be unclouded, and lead us toward the fortunate realms.

Thirdly, on arrival in the fortunate realms, it is customary for new deities to recollect their previous lifetime to see what good deeds caused them to arise in heaven. If there is a joyous emotion associated with those memories, it will bring special brightness and longevity in that new rebirth.

Last but not least, even arahants who have reached the point of enlightenment and are able to recollect previous existences, when they remember their previous acts of generosity, these will be accompanied by joy and radiance in a way that will inspire future generations of Buddhist practitioners.

Thus, whenever you have the opportunity to give a gift, you should allow yourself to be sparked to joy by your own generosity on that occasion, in a way that will inspire and motivate even greater philanthropy in your future. *<and continue with 'ending' at page 81>*

5

Open-hearted giving
& the rainclouds

According to the teaching of the Buddha, open-hearted giving brings benefits and can be developed on many levels.

Generosity is said to bring the character quality of nobility to the giver. As recorded in the Patta-kamma Sutta of the Aṅguttara-nikāya, the nobility of a household disciple comes from living with a heart free of the taint of stinginess, being open-handed and pure-hearted, delighting in self-surrender, welcoming being asked for favors and delighting in dispensing charitable gifts.

Furthermore in the Vuṭṭhi Sutta of the Itivuttaka the Buddha talked about open-hearted generosity on at least three

different levels – comparing the giver to three different sorts of raincloud.

The undeveloped generosity of the miser can be compared to a rainless cloud. This applies to the sort of person who does not give anything to anyone – no food, drink, clothing, vehicles, garlands, scents, ointments, beds, lodging or lamps – in support of renunciants, brahmins, the poor, destitute or needy.

A person who has started on the pathway of generosity can be compared to a cloud that rains *locally*. This applies to the sort of giver who gives only to *some* renunciants and brahmins, or *some* of the poor, destitute, and needy, but not to others.

A person who is a little further along the pathway of generosity can be compared to a cloud that rains *everywhere*. This applies to the sort of giver who gives to *all* renunciants and brahmins, and *all* the poor, destitute, and needy, regardless.

With the offering of the midday meal today, as part of the unbroken daily tradition in this temple extending back many years, I would like to congratulate all of you as being not only the clouds that rain everywhere, but as the *thunder*clouds. The monastic community would like to rejoice in all of your merits for always being responsive to requests, manifesting sympathy for all beings, distributing gifts with delight and with the words, "Give! Give!", encouraging others to do the same. Just as a cloud thunders, roars and rains, filling the plateau and plain, drenching everywhere with water, may all the good deeds of open-hearted generosity you have cultivated come back to you as torrent of health, wealth, happiness, fulfiment and nobility in life now and forevermore. *<and continue with 'ending' at page 81>*

6

Reasons for giving

According to the Buddha's teaching in the first verses of the Dhammapada, our intentions are the important precursor of every outcome, good or bad, that may occur in our lives. Even with the giving of a midday meal, some reasons for giving are *less* noble than others — that is, the more noble the intention behind an act of generosity, the more merit will be generated by the gift. Therefore to maximize the merit from giving, it is useful to be aware of the spectrum of intentions available, so that we can practice generosity for the best of reasons.

According to the Buddha's teaching in the Paṭhama Dāna Sutta of the

Aṅguttara Nikāya, some reasons for giving are self-centered while other reasons are nobler. As many as four self-centered reasons for generosity include giving because you want something in return, giving under duress, giving in order to pay back a debt or giving to procure a future favor. These four reasons are no more than ways of keeping up good relationships with the people around us. There is no real merit in such giving, any more than virtue signaling from politicians in order to win votes or stores boosting their sales by giving away free samples. Although some of these forms of giving are helpful or practical, because they lack purity of intention, they will fail to generate very much merit in the mind, and thus hold little interest for us in the pursuit of Buddhist perfections.

Instead of these, the Buddha advocated five nobler intentions for giving. He recommended giving for giving's sake — giving for the joy of it — perhaps because we are spontaneously inspired by a particular monk or to help out a group of stranded children by gladly paying for their transportation to the temple.

Secondly, the Buddha recommended giving out of sympathy for the monastic community. Knowing that monks are not supposed to be in the kitchen to make food for themselves, the sympathetic intention to alleviate the monks' hunger is a noble reason to give food.

Thirdly, the Buddha recommended giving as way to make yourself a more praiseworthy person – not out of hunger for praise, but because generosity is a behavior deserving praise by the wise.

Fourthly, the Buddha recommended giving to pave the way toward a heavenly destiny.

And last but not least, the Buddha recommended giving in order to improve the quality of the mind.

All these five reasons for giving are sufficiently noble to accrue merit in the mind. Certainly with the midday meal all of you have offered here today, the merit accrued will be strong because as well as improving the quality of the mind, the food is given out of sympathy for the monastic community, accords with what is praiseworthy, paves the path to heaven and is giving for giving's sake. <and continue with 'ending' at page 81>

7

The falling of rain

It is said that water lilies that float on the surface of a pond are made beautiful by two different things – one is the nutriment of the mud under the surface of the pond and the other is being watered by the rains that fall from the sky.

In Buddhism, the same principle applies to the flourishing of the monastic community which also depends on two important factors. The first factor is that the monks in the monastic community must be abundant with faith in the Triple Gem and put all their waking effort into striving to attain Nirvana. A second factor leading to the flourishing of the monastic community is that the monastic community must be well-provided for by a supportive lay community, to allow the

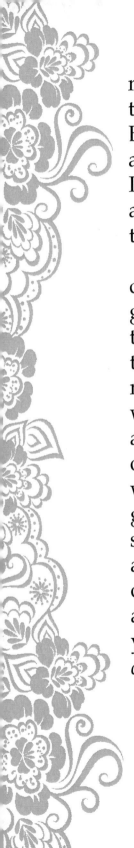

monks in the community to have the time to study and practice the teachings of the Buddha, training themselves to be truly a 'field of merit' to the people of the world. It takes both factors, the faith of the monks and the support of the laypeople to allow the monastic community to flourish.

Gifts to the monastic community, donated out of faith, that all of you have given here today, for the flourishing of the monastic community are like the rains that fall on fertile fields and are a great merit. They are the accumulation of wholesomeness which will come back to all of you givers in the form of fulfillment of wishes, whether it be abundance in worldly or spiritual ways. This rain of generosity from all of you will become a stream – from a stream to become waterfalls and rivers. From rivers it will flow into the ocean which will eventually come back to all of you as the conditions ensuring all of you can enter swiftly upon Nirvana. *<and continue with 'ending' at page 81>*

8

The joy of generosity

Many people find that the longer they have been meditators, the more they notice the effect of factors in their everyday life on the quality of their meditation practice. The Buddhist teacher Jack Kornfield once said, "Can you imagine settling down on your cushion for a peaceful meditation session after a full day of killing, stealing, and lying?"

By the opposite token, generosity brings joy to the giver as well as to the receiver. Indeed, generosity is characterized by the inner quality of letting go or relinquishing. It reverses the forces responsible for suffering. It is a profound antidote to the strong habits of clinging, grasping, guarding, and attachment that lead to so much pain and hardship.

As we learn to appreciate this, with an eye to improving our meditation, we

learn to give not only when opportunities present themselves, but we actually *look* for opportunities to give, and take delight in being asked to give. The Buddha taught the practice of generosity as the first step on the path, both in the Ten ways of cultivating merit and in the Ten Perfections, as a foundation for establishing an ethical lifestyle.

In regard to the fruits of generosity, the great Indian teacher Mahatma Gandhi once said, "The fragrance remains in the hand that gives the rose." Therefore we should not overlook generosity as the most important first step in our practice, the foundation on which we can build our actions, our meditation practice, and our spiritual journey – since in the words of the Buddha in the Itivuttaka:

> "Bhikkhus, if beings knew, as I know, the result of giving and sharing, they would not eat without having given. Nor would they allow the stain of meanness to obsess them and take root in their minds. Even if it were their last morsel, their last mouthful, they would not eat without having shared it, if there were someone to share it with."

<and continue with 'ending' at page 81>

9

The rewards of regular giving

Although it is widely understood that Buddhists believe in rebirth, not so commonly known is that Buddhists believe in different levels of heaven realm where beings who have had exemplary behavior in the human realm can live out their life in beautiful heavenly mansions for a long, but not eternal lifetime, when they pass on from the human realm. Merits such as offering a midday meal affect the way in which these heavenly mansions arise for the giver.

More than two thousand years ago, the scriptures record that, the Venerable Mahā Moggallāna was endowed with special mental powers by which, through meditation, he could visit the celestial realms, even without leaving his physical body. When he emerged from his meditation, he would relate what he had seen in those celestial realms for the

Buddha to hear. One thing he found in heaven was empty heavenly mansions where the owner had not yet taken up residence.

Our main teacher in Thailand, the Venerable Dhammajayo, explained why there should be empty mansions in the heaven realm. He said that generally for people who cultivate merits infrequently or on a one-off basis, the person has to die first, before their mansion will arise in the heaven realm through the power of the merit they have accumulated throughout their life. However, for those such as yourselves, who cultivate merits regularly, such as offering a midday meal every week, the mansion will arise in heaven, even though the owner of the mansion is still cultivating merit in the human realm, and will continue to increase in size, refinement and radiance, throughout the life of that person until, it reaches its final size at the end of their life and the owner can take up residence there.

Today, with the offering of the midday meal in accordance with your regular cultivation of wholesomeness, I can be sure that all of your heavenly mansions have grown yet brighter and larger in extent. *<and continue with 'ending' at page 81>*

10

Meaning of Pali blessings

Today, before you hear the blessing in the Pali language, I would like to take the opportunity to provide the English translation of the blessings we hear each time, so that for the English speakers here, you can have some idea of the meaning.

The blessing will start with *"Yathā vārivahā"* where the lead monk chants the verses of merit dedication for the departed with the words: Just as rivers full of water fill up the ocean, even so does the merit arising from these gifts, benefit the deceased. May whatever you wish for come quickly to fruition. May all your wishes be fulfilled as the moon on the fifteenth day, or as if by a wish-fulfilling gem.

The blessing continues with *"Ayudo"* – the verses of appreciation – with the

words: A wise person gives longevity, strength, clothing and knowledge. If a person gives happiness, later happiness will return to them. If a person gives longevity, strength, clothing or knowledge, they shall live a long life and be honored wherever they go.

Finally, the blessing ends with *"Sabbabuddhā…"* – the verses for the lesser universe of blessings – with the words: By the power of all the Triple Gem, by the power of the 84,000 sections of Dhamma, of all three sections of the Buddhist scriptures and of the Buddha's disciples – may all your diseases, dangers, obstacles and unfortunate omens be destroyed. May you enjoy increase of longevity, wealth, fortune, fame, influence, health and happiness without end. May any form of pain, disease, danger, enmity, sorrow, peril, distress, or obstacles, be overcome by this power. May you enjoy victory, success, wealth, safety, luck, happiness, strength, fortune, long-life, beauty, prosperity and fame – and have a hundred years of life, to enjoy a successful livelihood. *<and continue with 'ending' at page 81>*

11

Giving honor to the dead

Although many people are motivated to give a midday meal out of sympathy for the monastic community or because they would like to accumulate merit for themselves, others like to practice generosity in honor of loved ones of theirs who have already passed from this world.

For centuries, the bereaved have sought to do something more than remember or honor loved ones who have passed away. Often, they would like to ensure relatives who have passed on, are safe and well provided for, in their new existence. This has led to some strange practices down the ages such as (in India) the leaving of food on a dead person's grave so that they might not get hungry

or (in China) burning paper money so that loved ones may have a supply of cash in heaven.

If we were going to visit another country, we would have to make sure before departure that we have obtained the right currency for our trip. In the same way, when talking about the afterlife, the Buddha advised that not the possessions themselves, but merit alone will be of any use to those who have left this world. Thus, the giving of a midday meal is like converting physical gifts (the food offered) into merit that is meaningful for the loved ones who have passed away, by offering it to the monastic community. Some people have even referred to monks as being like the mail-carriers who ensure the delivery of the merit.

Thus, when we suspect that loved ones who have passed on are not happy in their new place – perhaps we have received visitations or bad dreams about them, it is wise to offer a midday meal in that person's name and dedicate merit by pouring water. Often afterwards, those loved ones will appear gratefully in our dreams, dressed in fine raiment and radiant with the merit they have received.

With the offering of the midday meal I am sure all the lucky deceased relatives of all who have had a hand in offering the midday meal will receive great merit, as a result of the pure intentions of all dedicating merit today. *<and continue with 'ending' at page 81>*

12

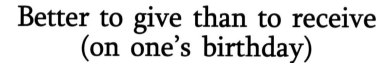

Better to give than to receive (on one's birthday)

There are some things that are universal truths that appear in the Buddhist scriptures and the Bible alike. One of these truths is that there are many reasons why it is better to give than to receive. This is especially the case for those who choose to offer a midday meal to monks on the occasion of their birthday anniversary, instead of just waiting to see what presents they will get or who will remember their birthday.

Giving instead of receiving has many advantages – for example, it makes you happier – since it has been proven that twice as many people who donated blood were happy, compared than those who didn't.

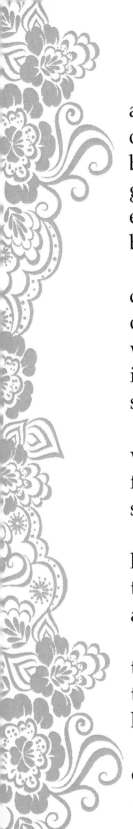

Giving communicates something about our worldview – because the opposite, hoarding, communicates the belief that there is only limited wealth to go around, and if we don't get it someone else will. There is research to show that being a giving person helps us live longer.

Giving increases our social connectedness – helping us perceive others more positively and charitably, while heightening a sense of *real* interdependence and cooperation in the social community.

Giving is contagious – with many real world examples of the idea of 'pay it forward' which have inspired others to show their generous side.

Giving gives your life meaning – healing the disconnect between who you think or say you are, and who you *actually* are.

Giving increases self-confidence and trust in those who receive our gifts, that they will do the *right* thing with what they have received.

Giving allows you to listen to others differently and look at your own resources without attachment.

Giving fosters contentment and promotes a universal good.

Finally, giving, especially within a marriage, helps to create lasting relationships – and more generally makes you a more likeable person.

Thus, with the offering of the midday meal today, especially for those offering food on their birthday, may this gift ensure that the year ahead for all of you, turns over a new leaf of prosperity, happiness, abundance and wealth for yourself and all those close to you. <and continue with 'ending' at page 81>

13

Almsgiving poem

Today I'd like to read to you an almsgiving poem commissioned by the Most Venerable Chao Khun Vithesbhavana-tham and written by one of our supporters in Manchester, England – Jeannette Slavinski – as a way of bringing to mind the merits arising from the offering of the midday meal here today.

There is a poem in the
heart of every human being.
The fruits of your labor,
are manifold.
Always make your intent,
compassionate, charitably bold.
A golden apple,
ripened by the sun.
A single crumb,

of bread
molded & risen by
the hand of time.
Refresh a holy palette with
God's own tear drops,
organic & divine.
Give love, give life,
give luck,
to a humble monk,
whom treads his rhythmic
barefoot journey, step by step,
of rainbow promises,
upon fragrant rose petals,
kindled by kind nourishment.
For it is better to
travel well
than arrive.
So strive to share the
poetic banquet of your heart.
The alms of plenitude,
sweetened by honey'd nectar.
And then to
dwell in the enchantment
of your own peace,
for there is no finer merit.

<and continue with 'ending' at page 81>

14

🎋 Ꮭ᎒ 🎋

Repetition doesn't reduce an action's worth

Sometimes we tend to assume that because something happens repeatedly, that it is ordinary or worthless. Especially where the offering of a midday meal here at the temple, is something that happens every day, it is important for us not to take such an act of generosity for granted.

In this connection, there is a record in the Samyutta Nikāya of a meeting between the Buddha and a reluctant giver called Udaya Brahmin. When the Buddha was in residence at Savatthī, one morning he took his robe and bowl, and approached the dwelling of the Brahmin Udaya on almsround. On that first morning, the brahmin Udaya filled the Buddha's bowl with rice without saying anything. On the second morning, again

the Buddha received alms from Udaya Brahmin, without the Brahmin saying anything. On the third morning the Buddha received alms from the Brahmin Udaya – but this time the Brahmin couldn't keep his mouth shut and complained, "This pesky monk is addicted to the taste of my food and just keeps coming back again and again."

In reply the Buddha commented "Brahmin – you have only been giving alms for three days and are you already complaining? Some things in this world happen repeatedly for a good reason – for example, farmers sow the seed repeatedly, the clouds shower us with rain repeatedly, plowmen plow the field repeatedly, grain ripens in the fields repeatedly, mendicants go for alms repeatedly, benefactors give repeatedly, when benefactors have given repeatedly, they go to heaven repeatedly, the dairy folk draw milk repeatedly, the calf goes to its mother repeatedly, the foolish do unwholesome deeds repeatedly, consequently they take rebirth repeatedly, once reborn, they have to suffer death repeatedly, once dead, they are taken to the cemetery repeatedly – but when one has obtained the path that leads to no further rebirth, having become replete in wisdom, one is no longer reborn repeatedly." Hearing these words, the Brahmin Udaya was renewed in his inspiration to support the monastic community and took refuge in the Buddha for the rest of his life.

As for us, although the cultivation of generosity may seem commonplace at our temple, my hope is that today you will see that such habitual pursuit of perfections will help protect us from all the forms of suffering that are so prevalent in our lives. <and continue with 'ending' at page 81>

15

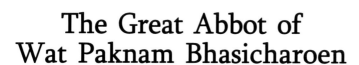

The Great Abbot of
Wat Paknam Bhasicharoen

When we think of the Great Abbot of Wat Paknam, who rediscovered the Dhammakāya meditation tradition, we recollect all the good deeds that he exemplified during his lifetime as a monk. The story I'd like to tell you today is about the strong connection, which the Great Abbot of Wat Paknam Bhasicharoen had to the practice of generosity and giving support to the monastic community.

This story goes back to the time when the Great Abbot was not yet an abbot, but was still a young monastic student of Pali language in Bangkok. In those days the monks who were students lived in great poverty. The monks went out for almsround every morning, but on many

days they could find no-one who wanted to give them any food. There was one particular occasion when the Great Abbot went on almsround for three days straight without receiving any food at all in his bowl. So he thought to himself, "Well, if I am going to die from starvation then at the very least, may I be an example to inspire those mean benefactors to give better support in the future for the monks who outlive me." On the third day he received a meager contribution in his almsbowl which was a little bit of rice and one banana. So before eating food that day he sat down to reflect on the food before eating and just at the time before he was about to take his very meager meal after three days with no food, there was a mangy dog which appeared beside him and he thought, "Well the dog probably has more need of food than I do." So with that thought he gave half of his rice and half of the banana to the dog. And he made a wish at that time that, "From this great sacrifice I've made even when I'm very hungry, even though I have not eaten for three days, but still I have the generosity to share with this stray dog, in the future, may I be able to establish a system whereby none of the monks in the temple will be in hardship from having to wait for their meal times anymore, so they can devote their time to the study and practice of the Dhamma and meditation." It turned out that the dog only ate the rice. It didn't even eat the banana, but the Abbot could not take back the banana because he could only take what had been offered to him.

However, through the power of that wish and through *that* great sacrifice when many years later he became the Abbot of Wat Paknam Bhasicharoen, it was the first temple in Thailand to establish what is known as a 'monastic kitchen' – a place where even without having to go on almsround, supporters could contribute sufficient for the monks to be able to have warm and healthy food every day without having to worry about their next meal.

And as a result of the support which the monks received through the farsighted-

ness and sacrifice of the Great Abbot of Wat Paknam, the temple went on to become well-known not only for excellence in the study of the Pali language, but also prowess in the practice of high-level meditation. *<and continue with 'ending' at page 81>*

16

The timely gifts of Añña-Koṇḍañña

New Year can be considered an artificial festival, simply the changing of a number on the calendar – but according to the Buddhist teachings, any occasion can be made into an opportunity for cultivating goodness by marking that occasion with merit making. Usually New Year's day is marked by an almsgiving ceremony to start the year as one means to go on, in accordance with a long tradition of timely giving in Buddhism.

The Dhammapada Commentary tells us that a long ago, in the time of Buddha Vipassī, there was a householder called Cula Kāla. Being a generous guy, he hired a large number of men for manual labor, and ordered grains of unripe rice to be

hulled, had it cooked in rich milk, adding ghee, honey, and sugar, and presented the rice thus prepared to the monastic community presided over by the Buddha. At the conclusion of the meal, the man made the wish, "By virtue of my gift of first-fruits may I be the first to win the foremost estate of all; namely, Arahatship."

When he went back to the field and looked at it again, he saw that the entire field was filled with heads of growing rice, bound together, as it were, in sheaves. At this sight he experienced the five kinds of joy. He realized, "I am indeed fortunate." From that time onwards he offered timely gifts of the first-fruits to the Saṅgha in a similar way at nine different stages of his harvest – when the rice was in the ear – when the rice was reaped – when it was in the sheaf – when it was in the stack – when it was in the rick – when it was threshed – when it was ground into flour – when it was measured – and when it was put away in the granary. Thus he bestowed the first-fruits of a single crop nine times. No matter how much he harvested to present as gifts to the monastic community he *was* always left with a plentiful crop.

Because he was always the first to give, ninety-one world-cycles later he was fulfilled in his wish to be the first to attain enlightenment under the dispensation of the Buddha Gotama in our own era under the name Añña-Koṇḍañña. *<and continue with 'ending' at page 81>*

Blessings
&
Endings

Ending of
Sammodanīya kathā

For the part you have played in offering the midday meal here today, the monastic community would like to rejoice in the merit of all joining today's ceremony. And at this time the monastic community would like to join our hands together in a gesture of prayer as we call down the spiritual perfections of the Triple Gem – the Buddha, the Dhamma and the Saṅgha, of the *paccekabuddha*s and arahants in Nirvana. Together with the spiritual perfections of all the root teachers in the Dhammakāya tradition – whether it be the Great Abbot of Wat Paknam Bhasicharoen who was the

rediscoverer of the Dhammakāya meditation tradition, whether it be our main teachers in Thailand – the Venerable Dhammajayo and the Venerable Dattajeevo. The spiritual perfections of all the monks in the monastic community who have conducted themselves in strict accordance with the monastic code of discipline throughout their time of ordination. The spiritual perfections of the Master Nun Kuhn Yay Maharattana Upasika Chandra Khonnokyoong, the founder of our main temple in Thailand.

May these spiritual perfections come together with the merits of generosity from offering the midday meal here today, with all of your past merits from participation in the temple activities down through the many years or decades that you have supported the temple, and the merits that you intend to cultivate further in the future. May all these spiritual perfections and merits come together as a bright clear sphere of merit at the center of yourself, that will help to protect you from all manner of misfortune, danger, suffering and sickness in life. At the same time, may these merits act as a magnet to attract into your life, all manner of good things – whether it be long-life, health, success, happiness, fulfillment, good complexion or quick-wittedness. Wherever you travel, may you have safety and protection in every place. Wherever you go, may you receive hospitality. When it comes to the time for you to meditate, may you be able easily to attain peace of mind, attain the inner sphere of the Dhamma, attain the body of enlightenment and eventually to reach the wisdom of Dhammakāya.

For those of you who would like to dedicate merit for loved ones of yours who have already passed, may these merits reach those loved ones wherever they have been reborn, to help to ensure for them, that they they enjoy happiness, radiance and ever increasing refinement in their new life.

At this time, the monks are about to give their blessing in the Pali language. For those of you who have prepared water for pouring in dedication to loved ones who have passed away, you can pour that water during the first part of the blessing. Otherwise, put your hands together in a gesture of prayer and make your own wishes for yourself or others as you hear the Pali blessing now.

Reflection on food before eating

<give blessing in Pali, chant Piṇḍapāta Dhātūpaṭikūlapaccavekkhaṇapāṭha>

At this time we close our eyes once again, and bring our attention back to the center of our body. We take this opportunity to reflect on the food before eating and also to offer the food in homage to all the Buddhas in Nirvana. We imagine the food we have offered today, or any food that we find easy to imagine, as if it is transformed to be crystal or diamonds in our mind's eye, at the center of our body – of a subtlety appropriate to be offered in Nirvana. And we bring this food in offering to the Buddha – not just one, but

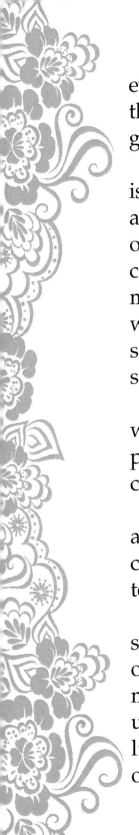

every Buddha in Nirvana more countless than all the grains of sand in all the four great oceans.

The merit of offering food to a Buddha is already immense, but when magnified and multiplied to the countless number of Buddhas in Nirvana, the merit is beyond compare. And as we receive the meritorious blessing from the Buddhas, we can make the wish to ourselves for success in our business lives or our studies, and harmony in our family life.

May we enjoy good health and long life without any sickness so that we may pursue perfection for a long, long time to come.

May we encounter only good, beneficial and wholesome things in our lives and continue to be inspired to practice the teachings of the Buddha.

May we be blessed with an unending stream of wealth to support our pursuit of perfection. At the same time may the merit help to vanquish any previous unwholesomeness still lingering in our lives which would otherwise lead to obstacles in life – whether it be anger, depression, boredom or despair which come as the result of our defilements.

May the merit facilitate our practice of meditation, allowing us to attain the true wisdom known to the Buddha with ease.

When it comes to time for us to leave this world, may our merit ensure we be reborn only in two worlds – the human realm and the heaven realms – until we can enter upon Nirvana.

We also dedicate the merit for the benefit of loved ones of ours who have passed away to bring them ever increasing happiness and refinement in the afterlife. *<pause>*

And having dedicated the merit in this way, we finish by saying the words '*Sesaṃ maṅgalaṃ yācāma*' together.

Appendices

3rd base

2nd base

4th base

1st base

5th base

7th base

6th base

The seven bases of the mind

How to meditate

Meditation is something which we already do in everyday life allowing us to focus on the task at hand — but the depth of meditation is superficial. The events around us in the world soon rob us of our attention and our concentration is gone. The mind that wanders outside our own body is the source of all types of suffering. By deepening our meditation until our mind comes to a standstill we can unlock the potential and unused ability within. We maintain a balance of mindfulness and happiness for ourselves bringing contentment and direction to life in a way not possible through any other technique.

(1) The sitting posture which has been found to be the most conducive to

meditation is the half-lotus position. Sit upright with your back and spine straight — cross-legged with your right leg over the left one. You can sit on a cushion or meditation mat to make your position more comfortable. Nothing should impede your breathing or circulation. Your hands should rest palms-up on your lap, and the tip of your right index finger should touch your left thumb. Feel as if you are one with the ground on which you sit. Feel that you could sit happily for as long as you like.

(2) Softly close your eyes as if you were falling asleep. Relax every part of your body, beginning with the muscles of your face, then relax your face, neck shoulders, arms, chest, trunk and legs. Make sure there are no signs of tension on your forehead or across your shoulders.

(3) Stop thinking about the things of the world. Feel as if you are sitting alone — around you is nothing and no-one. Create a feeling of happiness and spaciousness in your mind. Before starting, it is necessary to acquaint yourself with the various resting points

or bases of the mind inside the body (*see page 90*). The first base is at the rim of the nostril, on the right side for men and on the left side for women. The second base is at the bridge of the nose at the corner of the eye — on the right side for men and on the left side for women. The third base is at the center of the head. The fourth is at the roof of the mouth. The fifth is at the center of the throat above the Adam's apple. The sixth base is at a point in the centre of the body at the meeting point of an imaginary line running horizontally between the navel and the back and a second line between the two sides. The seventh base of the mind is two fingers' breadths above the sixth base. This base is the most important point in the body. It is the very center of the body and the point where the mind can come to a standstill.

(4) Feel that your body is an empty space, without organs, muscles or tissues. Gently and contentedly rest your attention at a point near to the seventh base of the mind — at the center of the body. Whatever experience arises in the mind, simply observe without attempting to

interfere. In this way your mind will become gradually purer and inner experience will unfold.

(5) If you find that you cannot dissuade the mind from wandering, then your mind needs an inner object as a focus for attention. Gently imagine that a bright, clear, crystal ball, the size of the tip of your little finger, is located inside at the center of the body. Maybe you'll find you can imagine nothing, but later you'll be able to see a crystal ball of increasing clarity. Allow your mind to come to rest at the very center of the crystal ball. Use the subtlest of effort and you will find that the crystal ball becomes brighter and clearer. If you use too much effort you will find that it gives you a headache.

(6) If you find that your mind is distracted by thoughts, you can dissipate the thoughts by repeating the mantra, *"Sammā-arahaṃ"* silently, as if the sound of the mantra is coming from the center of the crystal ball. Repeat the mantra over and over again without counting.

(7) Don't entertain thoughts in your mind. Don't analyze what's going on in

the meditation. Allow the mind to come to a standstill — that's all you need to do. If you find that you can imagine nothing, then repeat the mantra, *"Sammā-arahaṃ"* silently and continuously in the mind. If you find that you're not sure about the location of the center of the body, anywhere in the area of the stomach will do. Persevere because today's daydream is tomorrow's still mind; today's darkness is tomorrow's inner brightness; today's perseverance is tomorrow's fulfillment. Don't be disappointed if you find your mind wandering. It is only natural for beginners. Maintain focus continuously; keep your mind bright, clear and pure, and in the end, you will achieve your goal.

(8) Keep repeating the mantra and eventually the sound of the words will die away. At that point a new bright, clear, crystal ball will arise in the mind of its own accord. The crystal ball will sparkle like a diamond. This stage is called *paṭhama magga* (primary path). At this stage the shining crystal ball is connected firmly to the mind, and is seated at the center of the body. You will experience

happiness. With continuous observation at the center of this crystal ball, it will give way to a succession of increasingly purer bodily sheaths until it reaches the ultimate one called *"Dhammakāya"*, the highest level of attainment of supreme happiness.

About the author

Phra Nicholas Thanissaro has been a Buddhist monk for 24 years. With thirty years of meditation experience, he is a UK Complementary Medical Association qualified teacher of meditation. Affiliated with the Dhammakaya Foundation, he is also qualified as a school teacher and MBTI practitioner. As a scholar-practitioner, during his time as Associate Fellow at the University of Warwick, he was published widely in peer-reviewed journals on the formation of Buddhist identity in teenagers and continues to research the appeal of meditation in the West. He currently lectures in 'Living Buddhism' and 'Religious Individualization' at Claremont School of Theology, California and Willamette University, Oregon. His latest academic book, published in 2020, is entitled *The Intuitive Buddhist*.

Also by this author

Dhammadayada Chanting Book 130pp., 1989, 1994, 1999, 2003

Newcomers Guide to Wat Phra Dhammakaya 45pp., 1989

Meditator's Handbook 110pp., 1991

Buddhism into the Year 2000 (ed.) 348pp., 1994

The Life & Times of Luang Phaw Wat Paknam 160pp., 1996, 1998

Users-Guide Palitext version 1.0 68pp., 1996

Blueprint for a Global Being 88pp., 2000

The Buddha's First Teaching 257pp., 2002

Buddhist Economics 85pp., 2002

The Fruits of True Monkhood 187pp., 2003

Reforming Society means Reforming Human Nature 268pp., 2003, 2004

Second to None: The Biography of Khun Yay Chandra 174pp., 2005

GL101E Buddhist Cosmology (DOU) 145pp., 2005

Pearls of Inner Wisdom 114pp., 2006

A Little Book of Buddhist Chanting 96pp., 2006

MD101E Meditation I (DOU) 86pp., 2007

A Manual of Peace: 38 Steps towards Enlightened Living 466pp., 2005, 2007

Little Book of Buddhist Chanting (Woking tenth anniversary edition) 120pp., 2010

Start Meditation Today (3rd Ed) 40pp., 2016

Book & funeral sponsors

Dhammakaya International Meditation Center (Azusa)
Dhammakaya International Meditation Center Denver
Dhammakaya International Meditation Center Kansas
Dhammakaya International Meditation Center of New Jersey
Dhammakaya International Meditation Society of British Columbia
Dhammakaya Meditation Center Boston
Dhammakaya Meditation Center of Palm Beach
Dhammakaya Meditation Center Silicon Valley
Dhammakaya Meditation Center Tennessee
Florida Meditation Center
Georgia Meditation Center
Meditation Center of Chicago
Meditation Center of D.C.
Meditation Center of Texas
Minnesota Meditation Center
Oregon Meditation Center
Seattle Meditation Center
Wat Bhavana Mexico
Wat Bhavana San Diego
Wat Bhavana Toronto
- together with all 81 Dhammakaya Foundation branches in Thailand

Phra Kru Sothithamvites (Pratya Sotthijanyo)
Phra Mahā Sombat Indapañño
Phra Mahā Abhichart Vajirachayo
Phra Mahā Prasit Dittijayo
Phra Mahā Napasin Natthajayo
Phra Sophon Panyasophanoe
Phra Chutimavorakul
Phra Pepper Thanacaro

Jaisamarn Amree
Pakakrong Apisitpaisan
Wanida Asdondumrongchai
Viengkeo-Souchinda Borihanh
Sukum-Samon Boonjindasup
Ampika-Kenneth Carlson
Somporn Carter
Sakaorat Eve Chaisorn
Kaveesak Charoenjutarak
Terrie S. Chhu
Pakanang Chirachin
Keamchart Chumnanrob
Montatip Chumnanrob
Suganda Cluver
Martin Fedorski
Jane Godfrey
Tanawat Horsuwan
Rita Hunter
Charus Inkeo & Family
Pinthida Inkeo
Verapin Inkeo
Sarawin Intakanok
Tipsarene Intakanok
Gina Ishida & Family
Supaporn Jenarewong
Jonathan (Jonny) Liusuwan
Apsornsuda Kiatsilp
Steven Kheang
Wareerat Kleiber

Sayan Kongmuang
Amporn Kotchavong
Mylinh Lam O.D.
Pintip Metanai
Kanchana Ngamsuntikul
Serena Nimityongskul
Sue Palanchai & Family
Boonsak Pokpongkiat O.D.
Manee-Richard Prutz
Mia Rabaut
Varunee Racho & Family
Benjaporn Saejia
Teerayakorn-Sirichan Ruanglek
Suda Sawasdithep
Jeannette Slavinski
Serm Sribantaw
Umpawon Sripetchwondee
Chouywong Srisongkram
Jirada Sukata
Paula Sundara
Boondharika Supein
Sutheeta Thanasupharerk
Siriluck Thongaram
Michaël Van Steenkiste
Vassantachart Family
Verduzo Family
Sunee Vessri
Nataya Weraarchakul
Pritsadang Woralert